PORTALS REAL WORLD READING

BOUNCE

6

BILL LABOV

HOUGHTON MIFFLIN HARCOURT
School Publishers

Contents

No Pets on the Bus

Johnny

Linda

Miguel

Bip

What is in the box?

Bip.

What is a Bip?

Bip is not a "what." Bip is a "who."

7

Vick, vick.

What did Bip say?

Bip said,
"Where am I?"

Bip is in
the back!
Pick him
up! Quick!

Let him smell the jam.
I will pick him up! I will
get him back.

Mud on the Rug

We got a new rug. It's white.

Reina, do not get mud on my rug. NO mud on my rug.

So I did not walk on the rug. I did not sit on it. I did not go near it.

I did NOT get mud on it.

But Monday was wet.
Wet, wet, wet.

There was mud on the road.

Mud in the grass.

Mud on the walk.
Mud, mud, mud.

I came in. I took off my shoes.
No mud on my socks.

No mud on the rug.

Bo ran in. He put his big feet on the rug.
He sat on it. He got mud on it.
Mud, mud, mud.

Get out, Bo! You got mud on you
and MUD ON THE RUG!

So Bo got mud on Mom's rug. But Mom is mad at me.

I could tell on Bo, but I will not.

I'm not going to tell on my dog.

WAG
WAG
WAG

A PAIN IN THE NECK

This is my brother Jay. He is a real pain in the neck.

Jay blames me for everything.

Who let the cat sit on my bed?

Ray did it!

Jay did it!

Mom! Dad!
Jay did not get up.

Jay is still in bed.

Is Jay OK?

No, Jay is not OK.
Jay has a pain
in his neck.

I Hate That Hat

33

But who ate it?

I did.
I ate that hat.

I bit that big bite out of it. It made me mad.

LUKE'S BAD LUCK

Luke has a bad leg.
He can't run fast.
He won't win in a race.

But he's big for his age.
At bat he's an ace.

Saturday was a bad day.
Luke woke up late.

Yes, I AM late!

He broke his bike.

He broke his bat.

He ran to first.

He missed the bag.

Out!

We like Luke.
But he's no use to us.

Luke had bad luck.
He came home mad.

He saw a bug
on his big red rug.

I'll squish that bug
on my big red rug.

His mama said no.

Don't squish that bug.
It will bring bad luck.

I've GOT bad luck.

But he let it go.

Luke woke up.

SUNDAY

3

He got up on time.

He fixed his bike.

He got on his bus.

He got to his game.

Here he is.

US 8 GAME THEM 8

The game was tied.

Luke was up.

He hit that pitch.

BAM!!

Where did it go?
I can't see it.

Shopping with a Dollar

What's up, Del?

Hi, Ash. My uncle gave me a dollar, so I'm rich. I can go shopping.

Rich? A dollar is not a lot.

It's like ten dimes.

Will you get chips?

No way. My uncle said, "No chips. Chips are bad for kids."

Whose Phone Is This?

Somebody lost a cell phone. Whose phone is this? How am I going to give it back?

I lost my phone. How am I going to get it back?

Let me see the names on this phone.

MOM
555-5016
UNCLE DAVE
555-4555
AUNT SAL
555-5533

Let me see if Aunt Sal is at home. I can use Sal's phone to call my cell phone.

I'll call "Mom." She'll know whose cell phone it is.

RING! RING! RING!

Pick up! Pick up! "Mom" is not picking up. Well, I see she is not home.

I lost my phone, Sal. Can I use your phone to call it?

OK with me, Joan. Lots of luck.

Let me call "Uncle Dave."

Yes? This is Dave.

My name is Jane. I found a cell phone with your name in it. Do you know whose phone it is?

Nope. My kids have their cell phones with them.

RING!

Hello? Did you find my cell phone?

Yes, I did. How can I get it back to you?

I'm at a pay phone on Main and White.

Summer Job

SMITH'S MARKET
JUNE 21 cat food ⬇

I'm here to work, Mr. Smith. What can I do?

OK, Norma.
First, we'll just see if you can stack and how fast. This is kind of a test.

STACKING BOXES

Stacking is a real skill. Here are the rules. Use them to stack these boxes.

STACKING BOXES

1. If a box has a red spot on it, then you cannot stack it on a box with a white spot.

If a box has no red spot on it, then you cannot stack it on a box with a red spot.

2. If a box has no red spot on it, then you cannot stack it on a box with a red spot.

You will need a stepladder. Use these rules.

Cat Food

STAYING SAFE WHEN LIFTING BOXES

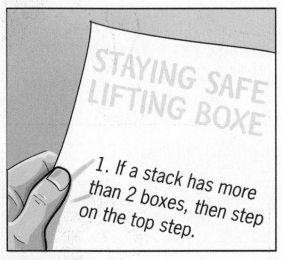

STAYING SAFE
LIFTING BOXE

1. If a stack has more than 2 boxes, then step on the top step.

2. If a stack has less than 3 boxes, then do not step on the top step.

Let me ask you something. Why do I still see boxes here?

Can't you read my rules?

I can read them, Mr. Smith, but they are a lot longer than they need to be.

STACKING BOXES

1. If a box has a red spot on it, then you cannot stack it on a box with a white spot.

2. If a box has...
it, then you cannot...
box with a red spot.

Monday

Hi Greg. What's going on?

I just wrote a story for Miss Gray. She asked me to read it to a second-grade class next week. I think the kids will like it.

Is that the name?

That's it. "Green Slime."

Let me see it. It's on green stuff?

Keep It Green

Well, I'm thinking green. Miss Gray ended class today by telling us we need to keep the planet green.

GREEN SLIME

Green Slime hides in shrubs and grass. If you step on it, it will grab you. It will suck you in.

Green Slime hangs from trees till you go by.

If Green Slime drops on you, they will not find you. Not ever!

Green Slime creeps out of the sea like a big green wave and takes you back with it.

Thursday

Where is Greg?

Friday

Greg's not on the bus?

Monday

Where did you go last week? I thought Green Slime had got you.

Keep It Green

Say, I hope you don't believe that stuff. I was at home with the flu.